Catholic Annulment

Spiritual Healing

Dennis and Kay Flowers

Liguori
ONE LIGUORI DRIVE
LIGUORI MO 63057-9999

Nihil Obstat:
The Reverend Mark Q. Fedor, JCD, M.Div.
Censor Deputatus

Imprimatur:
The Most Reverend Anthony M. Pilla, D.D., M.A.
Bishop of Cleveland
Given at Cleveland, Ohio, on 18 March 2002

Imprimi Potest:
Richard Thibodeau, C.Ss.R.
Provincial, Denver Province
The Redemptorists

ISBN 978-0-7648-0883-8
Library of Congress Catalog Number: 2002100278
© 2002, Dennis and Kay Flowers
Printed in the United States of America
14 15 16 17 18 / 10 9 8 7 6

Originally titled *Unlocking the Healing Power of Catholic Annulment,* © 1996.

Revised March 1, 2001

Scripture quotations are from the *New Revised Standard Version of the Bible*, copyright © 1989 by the Division of Christian Education of the National Council of Churches of Christ in the USA. Used with permission. All rights reserved.

To order, call 800-325-9521
www.liguori.org

About the Authors

Dennis, a Roman Catholic, met Kay, a divorced Protestant, at a storytelling conference in 1991. After dating for about eight months, Denny asked Kay to marry him. Before they could wed, the Catholic Church insisted that Kay have her first marriage annulled. After many angry tears, she went through the soul-searching process and was granted the freedom to marry Denny. Obtaining proper dispensation, they held their wedding in Kay's church, the Christian and Missionary Alliance Church. In an ecumenical ceremony, both Kay's minister and Denny's priest were there to witness their vows.

An interchurch couple who supports each other's faith traditions, Denny and Kay are members of the American Association of InterChurch Families. They attend each other's churches regularly and even serve in each other's denominations. In the Christian and Missionary Alliance Church, they work in the children's ministry. In the Catholic Church, they work in Cana II, a seminar for those being married for the second time, and in Couples Ministry, a one-on-one pre-marriage program for engaged couples, many of whom are also interchurch.

Denny and Kay are also professional storytellers who tell in tandem. As authors, they hold a number of copyrights for stories they have written. They are members of the Ohio Order for the Preservation of Storytelling, the National Story League, and the Apple Valley Storytellers.

They live on a small farm in Ohio, where they board horses and raise medicinal herbs and organic vegetables. They are certified equine massage therapists and Denny is also a licensed farrier.

Contents

Foreword

When Kay Flowers presented her marriage case to her local tribunal, she was told that it would accomplish two things: it would satisfy the requirements of canon law, and it would be a healing process for her. An avid reader and active in her own Protestant church, Mrs. Flowers devoured every book she could find about marriage annulments. She found that, although there are many books that attempt to explain the first part—the procedures used in a marriage nullity trial—there was no practical guide to spiritual growth and healing through the process. After her case received a favorable decision, and after her marriage to Dennis Flowers (a Catholic), the two decided to write this book to help others take advantage of the healing potential of the annulment process.

The couple enjoys an ecumenical marriage, and they are active in both of their churches. They belong to the American and International Associations of Interchurch Families, and they assist other couples in marriage preparation.

Why did they write their book? "A lot of people feel like they are the only ones who have done this and who have been through this process," according to the couple. They wanted to offer practical help to persons who submit a marriage case to a tribunal. At the heart of their book is a simple message: "Realize you are not alone, and realize that a closer relationship with Jesus will help you in this process." They wanted people to know what they've discovered by talking to many couples: "God is right there with you every step of the way" through a marriage nullity case.

Before writing this book, the Flowers' interviewed many couples who—like themselves —had gone through a tribunal case. The practical helps in the book come from the experiences and insights of these couples, and from the Flowers' own prayer life. It took them about two years to complete the book, and they emphasize that it is not just for Catholics. It can be a help for anyone who has a marriage nullity case before a tribunal.

Divorce is an inherently painful process. "It's great to know you can come through a process that is painful and difficult, and come out victorious on the other side because of the healing presence of God," Mrs. Flowers said. Her husband added that their book is different from other books about annulments in that it deals with spiritual healing and doesn't attempt to describe the procedures a tribunal follows in a marriage nullity case.

"Forgiveness," the authors say, "is the key to healing, but it can be done properly only by understanding your relationship with God." Mrs. Flowers adds, "The spirituality of the annulment process is all bound up with healing, but it makes sense only within a relationship with God."

Chapters entitled "Facing Reality," "Forgiving Others," "Forgiving Yourself," and "Closure" highlight the growth and healing that is possible through prayer. Other chapters provide immensely practical assistance: "Dealing with Your Children," "Non-Catholics," and "Support Helps."

Each year in the Diocese of Harrisburg, thousands of persons are involved in some way with an annulment process. Whatever role these persons play—whether a spouse who has petitioned the tribunal to investigate a failed marriage (the Petitioner), the spouse who is asked to respond to that request (the Respondent), or a witness in a marriage nullity trial—many questions usually accompany the process. Written for Petitioners and Respondents, this book offers help that is not bogged down in procedural jargon or canon law terminology. Instead, it keeps its focus clear to help a person discover a path to forgiveness, healing, and growth through the annulment process.

Often, the length and uncertainty of the process are as difficult for people as the memories that are relived in reviewing a marriage and offering testimony in an annulment case. A marriage nullity trial, legal in nature and bound up in procedural steps, is difficult for most people to comprehend. Puzzled by its complexity or lost in the legal jargon, some people focus exclusively on those elements of an annulment case. It is, however, still a work and ministry of the Church, and God's grace often works miracles through it by bringing healing, new strength, and the realization of God's empowering love. Mr. and Mrs. Flowers recognize this, and want to help others learn this truth as well.

It is not the purpose of an annulment process to bring healing, but instead to make a legal decision on the status of a marriage, based on carefully worded grounds of nullity recognized by the Church. Still, the process of reviewing one's life and marriage that often accompanies the start of a tribunal case can open the door to God's grace. This book can help in responding to the invitation of God to rediscover peace and joy.

If you are a party to a marriage nullity case, or if you know someone who is going through an annulment trial, this book can be a spiritual help.

Copies of this book have been sent to each parish in the Diocese of Harrisburg.

Very Reverend William J. King
Judicial Vicar, Diocese of Harrisburg
First published in *The Catholic Witness*,
February 25, 2000

Preface

In an age and a culture where we hear much about lawsuits, when people are consistently and constantly concerned about rights and legal redress, it is refreshing to read a book about healing. In a time when we all want to be able to blame somebody, anybody, for things gone wrong, we need a book about healing ourselves—healing that can come out of painful, sometimes hostile, and often guilt-laden relationships, or their termination. This is such a book.

An annulment is the determination that a marriage, which may have been entered into with the best of intentions and the greatest of hopes, had the seeds of its own death within it from the very beginning. It became a dream shattered. But because our religious beliefs revere matrimony as a sacred and irrevocable covenant in which God is intimately involved, it must be established that this particular union was somehow flawed from its beginning.

That brings up a flood of questions and emotions. How can you say my marriage never existed? How did I fail? Am I marked for failure forever? Am I a bad person? Is my partner, the parent of my children, a bad person? Why do I have to go through this whole process when I'm not even a Catholic? It's not fair. It's all legalism. And on and on.

This book is a view of that whole moment in our life which can bring contentment out of contention, healing out of hurt, sense out of nonsense, and peace out of pain. It may be the most important element of the whole process for our individual sanity. It may be a classic in our human struggle to combine the divine call to holiness with our fragile inadequacy. That is the hope of the authors.

Father John Mueller
Cleveland Diocesan Tribunal

Acknowledgments

We wish to thank Reverend Mark Q. Fedor and Reverend John Mueller for their encouragement and their knowledge of canon law which helped to structure this book.

We also thank Sister Mary Rose O'Connell and Elsie McGrath for their invaluable editorial expertise.

Special thanks go to Heidi Mack, whose patience and computer skills were essential to the original publication of this book.

Introduction

The Catholic annulment process can help Catholics and non-Catholics alike who seek inner healing from emotional abuse and painful memories after a broken marriage. However, because of its unique purpose and procedure, the annulment process itself carries an additional emotional drain. This can be so heavy a burden that many decide to leave the Catholic Church rather than answer the searching essay questions for an annulment.

In our research, we read several fine books about healing the pain of divorce, grief, and past memories, but we found none that dealt specifically with the capacity for healing in the annulment process. Perhaps it is this lack of information about the nature and purpose of annulments that leads people to misunderstand the intentions of the Church, and so to reject both the process and their Church.

Because we wish to pursue the potential for healing, our book does not deal with the actual process of annulment; this can vary to some degree from diocese to diocese and there are books and pamphlets that already provide this information. Our goal, for people who have already gone through an annulment as well as those facing the prospect of one, is to help them avoid bitterness by allowing God to heal their pain. With a growing faith and trust in a God who deeply loves them, they can learn to walk in the freedom God intended, the freedom for which Christ died.

We strongly advise taking the time to look up the Scripture verses cited in this book. God's Word is full of passages that show a divine longing to heal all hurting people. The Holy Spirit speaks through the Word of God, healing wounded emotions in the hearts of all who honestly seek to follow God.

We asked questions of priests and tribunal members, and interviewed other people who, like ourselves, had gone through the process. Many of their comments are quoted at the beginnings of each chapter. Names and certain situations have been altered to protect personal privacy.

As you seek peace and inner healing, may you experience more deeply the God who knows all about you and loves you beyond life itself.

PART ONE

PROCESS

CHAPTER ONE

Frequently Asked Questions

What is an annulment?

People enter into marriage with the best of intentions, but sometimes something is missing that is necessary for a lasting bond to be established. When this happens, it's clear that a legal marriage contract has been made but there is no spiritual content to the marriage, as God intended. There is no sacramental union, although there is a legal one.

The church (canon) law of the Roman Catholic Church assumes the marriage of two baptized Christians to be sacramental unless proven otherwise. The marriage of a baptized Christian to one who is not baptized is considered valid but not sacramental.

An annulment declares that this essential sacramental element was lacking in the marriage from the very beginning and therefore the couple was never actually joined together by God. If this is determined by a Tribunal, a decree of nullity can be granted and the persons are free to marry again.

Isn't that just a Catholic divorce?

No. Civil law is vastly different from church law. A divorce dissolves the legal contract of a marriage, whereas an annulment decides whether the spiritual content of a marriage was there or not. The annulment itself dissolves nothing. There must be a civil divorce *first*, before a church annulment can even be initiated.

Why is a Tribunal used?

In order to ensure justice for both Petitioner and Respondent, a Tribunal carefully reviews all the evidence and makes no moral judgments of right or wrong. The Tribunal does not seek to lay blame or to determine who was at fault. Their decision is based on the evidence given by witnesses and former spouses. The Tribunal deals with the spiritual aspect of the prior marriage in seeking to discover whether the sacramental element was present or absent right from the start. A Tribunal provides a structured process whereby marriage and divorce are examined within the confines of canon (church) law, rather than civil law. The rights and confidentiality of all parties are safeguarded.

Why is annulment necessary?

Marriage is a covenant that founds a partnership for life. When a couple marries, they must understand this lifelong bond and intend to remain faithful to each other. They must plan to be good to each other, putting each other's needs above their own. They must also be psychologically able and mentally mature enough to fulfill these intentions.

When baptized Christians marry with these intentions, the Catholic Church considers their marriage to have that essential sacramental quality that makes it an indissoluble union. In fact, the Church considers every marriage between baptized Christians to be valid and sacramental in nature unless it is proven otherwise. Without a decree of nullity, the marriage is still intact according to canon (church) law, even if civil law has granted a divorce.

Are there different types of annulments?

Not really. There is a standard form consisting of essay questions, and a shorter form for Catholics whose previous marriage ceremony was performed outside the Catholic Church or without proper dispensation from canon law.

What is the cost?

The fee suggested varies within dioceses, but it is normally only about half what the actual annulment costs. Depending on your ability to pay, the fee may be lessened or waived entirely.

How long does it take?

It depends on the Tribunal's backlog of work and the complications of your case. It can also hold things up if witnesses are slow to respond, or if the former spouse refuses to cooperate. Generally, it takes anywhere from six months to two years.

Either party may appeal the case if the outcome is not the one hoped for. This additional process can add months or years to the initial annulment.

What if I'm already remarried?

See your priest and discuss what action needs to be taken. You may need to go through the entire annulment process or just fill out a form. The Catholic Church is very concerned that all its members become reconciled and be welcomed at all the sacraments, so that all may enjoy the benefits of full communion.

What is a procurator?

This is the person who helps you initiate the annulment process, and does the paperwork and legwork necessary to place your case before the Tribunal of your diocese. Procurators can be priests, nuns, pastoral ministers, or anyone who has been trained in this area. In some dioceses they are called advocates or case assessors, or they may not have an official name at all.

Can I go ahead with the wedding before I receive notification about my annulment status?

The Catholic Church considers all marriages between baptized Christians to be valid and binding for life until proven otherwise. Without a declaration of nullity, you would not be free to remarry. It is wise to hold off on setting a wedding date until you receive a favorable decision.

If my previous marriage is annulled, does that mean my children are illegitimate?

Absolutely not! Annulment deals only with the religious laws of a marriage, not the civil laws. It does not affect the status of your children in any way. A declaration of nullity does not mean a previous marriage never existed, only that it did not have the spiritual content to make it sacramental. The Church considers your children to be legitimate offspring of your previous marriage. All civil laws, such as child support and custody, are still in effect as well.

What if I can't find witnesses?

In some rare cases, this happens. If the divorce happened a long time ago, it may be difficult, if not impossible, to locate witnesses. They may have moved, or even passed away. Find a sympathetic priest who can guide you. There may be a pastoral solution that will work for you.

What if I disagree with the decision of the Tribunal?

You have the right to appeal all the way to Rome. If you decide to appeal, you will need to pay a further fee to cover the costs. However, every favorable decision is already appealed by being sent to another tribunal for review, to see if they agree with the original decision. There is no fee for this automatic appeal.

Why does a non-Catholic have to get an annulment in order to marry a Catholic?

Every marriage, Catholic or not, is considered a valid union. A marriage between two baptized Christians is considered sacramental—a promise "till death do us part"—unless proven otherwise. You can have only one sacramental marriage at a time. Therefore, the Church needs to investigate the prior marriage to discern whether it was truly sacramental in nature, the way God intended marriage to be. If it was not, it can be annulled and the persons involved are considered free to enter marriage again. If, however, the previous marriage is deemed to have been sacramental, then in actuality the marriage still exists in the eyes of the Church and the persons involved are not free to remarry.

There would be serious spiritual consequences for a practicing Catholic who married a person without the Church's blessing. A Catholic who marries a divorced person without benefit of annulment cannot fully participate in the Catholic faith and cannot receive all the sacraments. This would be a detriment to the Catholic's spiritual growth.

CHAPTER TWO

Why Have the Annulment Process?

"My first marriage was a disaster, so when I met the man who was to become my fiancé, it was like an opportunity to start life over. But when we went to the priest, he said I had to have my first marriage annulled. Why wasn't my divorce enough?"

"I can't believe I have to make contact with my ex-wife and her family again! They all hate me! If the Tribunal believes everything they say, I'll be branded for life!"

"Look, I don't want to answer a bunch of highly personal questions that are going to be read by some nosy priests! Who do they think they are, to pass judgment on me? They don't even know me! They haven't gone through what I've experienced!"

"What exactly does an annulment mean—that I wasn't married at all? I've got three kids to prove it!"

The annulment process is a time-consuming, generally painful process to go through, especially if you've already experienced a bitter divorce in the courts. It may seem to you that obtaining an annulment from the Church is *worse* than getting another divorce. You answer dozens of essay questions about every detail of your failed marriage. You submit names of witnesses who give their opinions about your marriage. Your former spouse also gets a chance to tell the other side. All this gets sent to a Tribunal of complete strangers who make a final pronouncement on whether or not the Church holds your marriage binding. The whole procedure seems intrusive, frustrating, even frightening.

If you are the Petitioner (the one seeking annulment), you may be fuming that the Catholic Church demands you go through this lengthy process. Who has time for all this soul searching? Is it worth all the legal hassle just so you can remarry with the Church's blessing? If you are the Respondent (the one who was notified of the annulment proceedings), you may also be reluctant to drag up all the painful memories again just to satisfy the Catholic Church's religious (canon) law. Wouldn't it be better to leave the past alone and simply let everything fade away with time?

Why does the Catholic Church demand that its members go through this process? And why is annulment also required for divorced persons of other faiths who wish to marry a Catholic?

These are fair questions. The answers are related to the Catholic Church's view of marriage as a sacrament, a vocation, a covenant, and an indissoluble union. If there seems to be a record number of annulments at this time in history, it is not that the Church is caving in to demand. Rather, it is because so many members are marrying without a clear understanding of the requirements for true Christian marriage.

The Catholic Church views a sacrament as an outward sign instituted by Christ to give us grace. In the holy sacrament of marriage, the couple becomes ministers to each other of God's grace, the grace needed to live out their lives as a loving married couple in God's service. This grace comes from God through the Holy Spirit to the couple, through the pronouncement of their wedding vows, and continues throughout their marriage. In essence, they become the sacrament to each other.

1 Peter 4:10 explains that we are stewards of God's grace, and Hebrews 4:16 invites us to ask boldly for the grace that Christ has made available to all believers. In a sacramental, Christian marriage, each spouse relies on God's help, asking for and receiving grace as it is needed so that a valid, caring partnership is formed. God has an active part in their marriage. The way that Christians view marriage, then, is not the same way most of the world views it.

Marriage between two baptized Christians who are not Catholic has the same validity. The Catholic Church recognizes the validity of that marriage as a sacrament in the same way that baptism is recognized as a sacrament regardless of the denomination. This is why the Catholic Church wants to verify the validity or sacramental nature of any former marriage, Catholic or not, when annulment is involved.

Marriage is also a vocation, a calling. Before Christians decide to marry, it would be helpful to first look at whether God is calling them to a married vocation. Given their specific gifts, shortcomings, and personalities, would they serve God better married or single? Heartbreak can sometimes be avoided by carefully considering not only what you would *like to do*, but also what you think God is *asking of you*.

When viewed as a binding covenant that is indissoluble, marriage within the Catholic Church becomes a matter not to be taken lightly. In a marriage covenant, both spouses have to be willing right from the start to serve God in each other: to look after each other's needs first; to be willing to work out conflicts and talk over grievances; to allow God to work in them and in their marriage; and to be open to life and children, and to raise them Christian by example, deed, and instruction.

This is what the Tribunal looks for when an annulment is sought: Was this "content" ever present in the marriage? If there was no "content," can it be said that the marriage was a loving, binding contract, as God intended?

In other words, couples who feel called by God to have a permanent, indissoluble marriage covenant will need the free-flowing grace of God in their lives in order to make their marriage sacramental in nature. They should be able to say that, of their own free wills, they are making a covenant before God to love, honor, cherish, obey, and be faithful to each other until death, no matter what happens. Willingly, they agree to place each other's needs and the needs of their family before their own, to try to resolve conflicts, to support and help their spouse's relationship with Christ. In short, they are promising to love each other with God's sacrificial, unconditional love. Such a covenant before God is a sacrament, and indissoluble, as stated in Mark 10:9. In the sight of God, and with God's blessings, the Catholic Church joyously joins the bride and groom who come to the altar with these loving intentions.

As God's chosen ones, holy and beloved, clothe yourselves with compassion, kindness, humility, meekness, and patience. Bear with one another and, if anyone has a complaint against another, forgive each other; just as the Lord has forgiven you, so you also must forgive. Above all, clothe yourselves with love, which binds everything together in perfect harmony. And let the peace of Christ rule in your hearts, to which indeed you were called in the one body.

COLOSSIANS 3:12-15

But suppose a bride or groom (or both) comes to the wedding altar with less permanent, less caring intentions, either conscious or subconscious. Already, that marriage harbors preexisting conditions that can prevent the couple from making a binding commitment. Such a seriously flawed marriage does not have the proper foundation to be sacramental in nature.

Consider this: Can God's grace flow through a spouse who is verbally or physically abusive? Can a husband and wife truly be a sacrament toward each other when both are absorbed with their own interests, neither showing essential concern for the welfare of their mate? What about the young people who find themselves pregnant and are pressured by their parents to marry? There is an obvious question as to whether God has indeed joined these individuals.

Then there is the well-meaning couple who harbors serious reservations about total commitment to their marriage. Their love is conditional, based on human standards. They expect to love each other "as long as" there is physical attractiveness, "as long as" there is plenty of money, "as long as" their wants are met. There is a strong feeling of impermanence right from the very start.

This is not to suggest that the Holy Spirit cannot work in the above situations. It is just that God's grace has difficulty flowing in such marriages because it is blocked.

The annulment looks at whether the initial consent was flawed and therefore the expected marriage bond did not occur. It is not concerned with pointing out blame, or judging who was right or wrong. It is not—nor should it be looked at as—a kind of religious divorce decree. A divorce says that where there once was a marriage contract, it is now dissolved. An annulment says that because the marriage had no content as God intended, there was no contract to begin with. The annulment does not "dissolve" the former marriage, as a divorce does.

The two-fold purpose of an annulment is to discern whether or not this marriage was truly binding in nature, and then to help the wounded parties understand what happened, so they can be healed of their past pain and able to avoid making the same mistakes in their future marriage. The probing essay questions can help assess personal readiness for marriage by zeroing in on the true underlying problems, not just the symptoms. For instance, one spouse may have been an alcoholic and that can cause a myriad of problems, but were the true reasons for the excessive drinking ever discerned? Did either spouse ever go for counseling? Is substance abuse still evidenced? Answering the annulment questions honestly can point out where both petitioner and respondent need guidance.

After uncovering and facing initial problems, and each person's contributions to those problems, both former spouses benefit. Healing from past mistakes and painful memories will bring new freedom to accept and give God's forgiveness and grace so that the next marriage can be a true sacrament in the fullest sense of the word.

But why is an entire Tribunal process necessary? Why can't the Church let its members decide for themselves? Why can't the Church accept their divorces and let them begin a new life with a new partner?

Human nature has an incredible potential for deceit by rationalizing its own actions. One spouse may decide the marriage was sacramental but the other may decide it was not. How would this situation ever be resolved? With the use of an outside source, such as a Tribunal, more than one person is looking at the annulment essays. The entire situation is better discerned and less likely to be a matter of opinion. The Tribunal seeks out whether there was true content to the marriage, but no moral judgments are made. Rather, the evidence for nullity is weighed carefully, as outlined in canon law.

What if the annulment questions are answered dishonestly? Some may fear false accusations and harsh treatment from former spouses or in-laws. Even if they *seem* to "get away with it" in this life, remember, there is a God who judges all things with righteousness and wisdom. It may be possible to deceive the members of the Tribunal, but no one will be able to deceive God at the final judgment. "So then, each of us will be accountable to God" (Romans 14:12). Those who answer the essay questions with an air of self-justification are only fooling themselves. By refusing to face reality, such deceivers find the same unresolved problems following them into new relationships.

In Barbara Shlemon's book, *Healing the Wounds of Divorce*, there is an excellent chapter on annulments. She shows great insight and depth in her assertion of the annulment's helping to resolve inner conflicts as one contemplates sensitive issues and hidden motives.

An annulment need not be dreaded nor feared. It is not the end of the world; it can be a marvelous beginning. The child of God can claim this wonderful promise found in Jeremiah 29:11: "For surely I know the plans I have for you, says the LORD, plans for your welfare and not for harm, to give you a future with hope."

CHAPTER THREE

Finding a Procurator

"It was really rough on me. My procurator told me to take it in small doses, only as much as I could handle for that day. That helped a lot."

"The priest we chose as our advocate handed me this thick package and told me to fill it out. He said he would take care of all the legal work. It was so cold."

"My case assessor made sure I understood what I was doing and why. He answered all my questions, and was kind and patient, even when I cried in his office."

"I was intimidated by the personal nature of the written work. I was so glad someone else was going to handle taking it to the Tribunal."

Your procurator can be a priest, deacon, or any other lay pastoral minister who is familiar with canon law and has been trained to guide petitioners through the annulment process. This person will assist you, get the materials you need, write a cover letter introducing you and your case, and submit your finished written work to the Tribunal.

Your diocese may call this person an advocate or a case assessor, or may not even have a title for the person who handles annulments. In the Cleveland Diocese, where this book was written, the person who handles annulment cases is called a procurator. For convenience, the word "procurator" will be used in the rest of this book.

Finding an appropriate procurator can be like finding the best recipe for chocolate cake. Everyone has personal preferences. You may like a procurator who is brisk and to-the-point, who will get the job done with maximum efficiency. If you're the more sensitive type, you may need more emotional support, more time to reflect. Maybe you just want a good listener with a sense of humor. Laughing when you feel like crying can be very healing.

Usually the procurator will be from your own parish, but you may want to do some shopping around to find just what you need. If your personalities clash, you may complete the annulment questions in anger, in deep guilt, or even flippantly, in which case the annulment process will be unable to do its healing work in your life because you will not have given it your best shot. Decide what qualities you want in a procurator, and then look for someone who has these characteristics. If no one springs to mind immediately, ask around your parish or at other churches until you find someone who will be able to support you through this most difficult process.

At the very least, a procurator should be kind, knowledgeable, and spiritual: kind because you will need a sympathetic friend who will encourage you and not grow impatient with your temper or your tears; knowledgeable because he or she must know canon law, the annulment process, and a bit of psychology, in order to guide you through the stages of healing; and, most importantly, spiritual because you need to hold on to God most tightly when you are hurting the most. Sometimes you have to hear this truth from someone else before you can actually believe it for yourself. Your procurator should be the first one to point you to God's abiding love and concern.

Keep in mind that very few procurators have actually gone through the annulment process for themselves. Someone who has not gone through a divorce can never truly understand the debilitating hurt, anger, and rejection you may have experienced. In the same way, it will be impossible for your procurator to completely empathize with your feelings during the annulment process. However, a well-chosen procurator with the compassionate heart of Christ can do much for you on your road to healing.

O LORD, you have searched me and known me. You know when I sit down and when I rise up; you discern my thoughts from far away. You search out my path and my lying down, and are acquainted with all my ways. Even before a word is on my tongue, O LORD, you know it completely. You hem me in, behind and before, and lay your hand upon me. Such knowledge is too wonderful for me; it is so high that I cannot attain it.

PSALM 139:1-6

Understand that God is right there with you, loving you through your worst times.

Chapter Four

Support Helps

"I don't know how I would have finished the written essays if my fiancée hadn't typed everything up for me. She was such a comfort to me."

"My procurator must have been tired of hearing me rail against the Church for putting me through this. She told me next time I saw the priest to tell him what I thought. I made an appointment, and yelled at him for forty minutes! He was so receptive and understanding—to my amazement! I think just getting all that rage out of my system was the first big step toward healing."

"I went to the park to write. It was quiet and peaceful there. I could get away from the environment where it all happened. It felt safe and neutral."

"My girlfriend probably wanted to take the phone off the hook sometimes, but she was always there for me."

Your circumstances may warrant support. You may feel you need something a little extra to help you through the writing and the waiting period. This is normal.

You may find solace in your pet. It has been researched and recognized by the scientific community that stroking a cat actually lowers blood pressure. When a phone conversation with her former mother-in-law sparked frustration, one woman ran out to the pasture and cried on her horse's neck for comfort. If you find the pressure of reliving painful memories too much for you, a romp in the backyard with your dog may be just the release valve you need.

Nature may provide the quiet atmosphere you need for inner healing. Getting away from the phone, the kids, the laundry, the desk work, the bills, and everyday hassles can help you think more clearly: a walk along the beach, a hike through the deep forest, canoeing, camping, biking—anything that gets you outdoors and clears your mind. Then you may be able to put your thoughts down on paper without the writer's block of day-to-day interruptions.

Spending time alone can be refreshing and calming. Children are not the only ones to benefit from a personal time-out. You may want to take a short trip, or arrange to use a friend's vacant summer cottage.

There are also weekend experiences for the divorced organized by the Catholic Church, as well as many kinds of retreats, and these can lessen stress in your life. Contact your diocesan Marriage and Family Life Office for more information. Generally, these retreats are recommended only for those who have been divorced for at least a year.

Most people find it easier to answer the annulment's probing questions in a private setting, away from noise and distractions. This may be next to impossible with a family, but if you're creative, you'll find a quiet place to work, such as the library, so that you can give your full attention to the importance of the written essays.

It might be helpful to have in view a specific item that gives you comfort. One woman lit candles each time she sat down to work on the annulment questions. You might want a crucifix, your Bible, or a favorite picture to glance at as you work.

Everyone should have at least one close friend to confide in—a college buddy, family member, next-door neighbor. This is a time when you really need someone to listen to you, to help you remember details, to let you vent your emotions freely, perhaps even to read or type up what you have written.

It may surprise you to find your future spouse to be this best friend. Often, after reading what you have gone through, your future spouse will be better prepared to understand your feelings and deal with your needs as they arise. Enlightened understanding and true forgiveness can cement your relationship firmly together as you work out your new life as husband and wife.

The church building itself can be a comfort, as you spend many hours there in prayer. It can be a cleansing gift to listen to God's love and feel God's comforting arms around you.

If you are a remarried Catholic seeking reconciliation, knowing that the annulment process can bring you back into full communion with your Church is extremely healing. You know you are doing what is right in the sight of the Church and will once again be welcomed back into complete communion at the Eucharist. This can be a joyful release of emotion, a true spiritual healing.

Like some, you may feel the need for counseling and therapy. This is wise where there is deep wounding. If you break your leg, you go to a doctor to get it fixed. A broken heart and crushed spirit deserve no less attention, and God understands this. The world you live in is not a simple one; there are many complexities that make up relationships, and even more that break them up.

Perhaps you would like a trained counselor to help guide you through intricate parts of your life, to enable you to see what went wrong in your marriage. Contact your diocese. Through the Marriage and Family Life Office or the Office of the Tribunal, a good counselor may be found for you. If not, ask around. It might surprise you how many people have had therapy.

One more thing. A Catholic counselor may understand the impact of the annulment questions and so be better able to guide you through the process to healing. If you choose this route, be sure you feel comfortable enough with your counselor or therapist to delve into your past memories with honesty.

You may think the writing of so many essays is torment enough, but many people find it revealing to keep a journal. A private diary may open up your memory bank for the essays you will be writing; it is also a safe place for venting anger, frustration, and discouragement. Whatever you write down is just between you and God. You may also be able to trace the steps of healing through your journal, as you put down on paper your deepest inner feelings. It can be a source of enlightenment for you to read months, or even years, later, to see how far you have come in your spiritual walk with Christ.

Your church may have a support group of its own or you may want to start one. One woman found compassion and spiritual uplifting from the charismatic group she attended. Her friends and spiritual leader became firm steppingstones on which she could stand in safety as the dark waters of her troubled life swirled around her feet. She was able, with their help, to face the difficult times with full confidence in God's love and concern for her. "Cast all your anxiety on him, because he cares for you" (1 Peter 5:7).

Volunteer work or ministering to shut-ins can be a valuable outlet for creative healing. Giving to others is a way of healing yourself, of refusing to be stifled by your own pain, of bearing one another's burdens in Christian love. Galatians 6:2 encourages you to help others and share their burdens and sorrows: "Bear one another's burdens, and in this way you will fulfill the law of Christ." Whether you shovel snow for an elderly person, pray for the sick, or pass out blankets for the homeless, you are showing love for your Lord if you do it for his sake and in his character. "Truly I tell you, just as you did it to one of the least of these who are members of my family, you did it to me" (Matthew 25:40). In helping others less fortunate, you will distract yourself from focusing on your own pain. This can be a way of starting your own recovery.

The Healing Power of Doing Good—the Health and Spiritual Benefits of Helping Others, by Allan Luks with Peggy Payne, is a good book to read if you are interested in this aspect of emotional healing. The authors cite many avenues of service, and pull anecdotes from the lives of people who have benefited through their choice to help others.

As mentioned in the previous chapter, your procurator can be a real friend to you in your need. A procurator is a kind of buffer zone between the Tribunal and those seeking an annulment. You may never meet a member of the Tribunal, and it is easy to become bitter against these strangers who are making decisions on your life. Your procurator is the safety net under your tightrope as you walk through the annulment process. Keep balanced and on the right track by talking out your frustrations and finding answers to your questions.

Spending time quietly reading God's Word can be a wonderful source of comfort. "For whatever was written in former days was written for our instruction, so that by steadfastness and by the encouragement of the scriptures we might have hope" (Romans 15:4). The Psalms especially have been found to be a true strength for those seeking solace down through the ages. Meditating on the daily lectionary readings can bring peace of mind.

Certainly, talking to God and spilling out your anger, despair, pain, and feelings of emotional abuse can be exceptionally beneficial on your journey toward inner healing. God knows what you're experiencing.

Have you been rejected? So has God! "The more I called them, the more they went from me.... Yet it was I who took them up in my arms.... I was to them like those who lift infants to their cheeks" (Hosea 11:2,3,4).

Has your love been spurned? God understands. "How often have I desired to gather your children together as a hen gathers her brood under her wings, and you were not willing" (Matthew 23:37).

Have you felt alienated? So has God! "He came to what was his own, and his own people did not accept him" (John 1:11). As your Creator, God knows all about you. Because Jesus lived a human life on Earth, he has tasted the bitterness of life as well. "For we do not have a high priest who is unable to sympathize with our weaknesses, but we have one who in every respect has been tested as we are, yet without sin" (Hebrews 4:15).

God *does* understand. Time spent in prayer is never wasted time; it is the most valuable thing you can do. Rely on God for the strength and wisdom you need.

Possibly one of your best sources for support, however, is from someone who has already obtained an annulment and found healing in the process. This is a person who can truly empathize and encourage you. In your trials, God comforts you so that you in turn can then truly comfort others. "Blessed be the God and Father of our Lord Jesus Christ...who consoles us in all our affliction, so that we may be able to console those who are in any affliction with the consolation with which we ourselves are consoled by God" (2 Corinthians 1:3,4). A person who has once walked where you are now walking has come through the shadows victorious. Seek out a person like this through your parish's couples ministry or Cana programs.

Find the help and guidance you need, and keep relying on God's strength to get you through to the other side of healing.

CHAPTER FIVE

Non-Catholics

"Why do I have to follow their rules? I'm not Catholic! It's such a power play! Is all this really necessary?"

"My first time as a procurator, I was flabbergasted when I learned from this wonderful Methodist man that the priest had told him he had to get his first marriage annulled before he could marry his Catholic fiancée! I told him he must really love her to go through all that for her."

"I've already had therapy to get over the pain of my divorce. Now I feel like the Catholic Church is ripping out all my stitches and I have to go through it all over again! Why?"

"I already feel so alienated because I can't take communion with my fiancée. All this red tape just makes matters worse."

Admittedly, when you come from a non-Catholic background, an annulment seems cruel and unnecessary. You've gone through enough pain and suffering because of your divorce, and you don't want to deal with it again.

If you let it, the annulment can help eliminate some

of your pain by giving you the chance to heal from your hurtful past. In addition to satisfying the legal aspect of the Church's canon law, the annulment process is also offered as an opportunity for healing and reconciliation with your past. Unless the conflicts of your previous marriage are confronted and resolved, it will be difficult, if not impossible, for your next marriage to be joyful and peaceful.

Combined with an accepting attitude, the annulment questions can be a gift of great value in preparing you for future relationships and for healing the wounds of past ones, including those of your own family. Unresolved and unforgiving anger can turn into destructive behavioral patterns. These harmful habits and reactions are detrimental to the freedom and joy God wants for you and has provided for you in Christ. Emotional baggage drags you down. It prevents you from becoming the best person you can be. It keeps you from becoming the best spouse you can be. Through the annulment process, the Catholic Church can help you move toward inner healing.

Feel free to ask questions of the priest or your procurator. Feel free to vent your anger. Feel free to seek more sympathetic help if you feel you are not being dealt with in a compassionate way. Annulment can be an exhausting process, especially when you are understandably reluctant about coming under the law of a church that is not your own.

It may help to look at it this way. The Catholic Church is a huge institution with authority in both religious and political areas; Vatican City is considered its own country. If you were going to Germany to marry a German citizen, you would be subject to the laws of that country even though you may be a valid, upstanding citizen of another country. The nation of Germany has a right to state the conditions under which one of its citizens may marry. You have a right to agree or disagree, but it remains that you still must obey the German laws.

When you marry a Catholic, you're getting a package deal. Just like in-laws, the Catholic Church is included in your marriage, and this doesn't have to be bad. The Catholic Church assumes spiritual authority for each of its members. Therefore, when a Catholic decides to marry, the Church wants to ensure that both partners are truly free to marry.

Every marriage is presumed valid unless proven otherwise and there can be only one covenant, or binding, marriage at a time. A marriage between two non-Christians or a Christian and a non-Christian, though not sacramental according to church law, would still be considered valid and binding.

In Catholic thought, there are special sacramental graces God provides for a marriage between two baptized people. God's prerogative to act is not limited in *any* marriage, however, so if the intended spouse was married and is now divorced, the Church needs to determine whether the consent that was given in that marriage was indeed binding. If it was not, then the intended spouse is free to marry the Catholic with the blessing of the Church. If, however, the marriage was deemed binding, then the intended spouse is still married according to canon law, the religious law of the Church. If the Catholic marries this person without the first marriage being annulled, the Church teaches that this couple is considered to be in an "irregular situation" involving a state of sin.

In his address to the members of the 1997 Pontifical Council for the Family, Pope John Paul II stated that Catholics in an "irregular situation" contradict the faithful unity of love between Christ and his Church and therefore cannot be admitted to the Eucharist. Since this sacrament constitutes spiritual nourishment and is a vital, sacred part of Catholic worship, the danger to the Catholic's spiritual growth is clear in this case. The Church wishes to protect its members to the best of its ability.

As a non-Catholic, you will also be under this protection, in a sense. An annulment is the Church's way of agreeing with you that your previous marriage was seriously flawed, that it did not fulfill the essential requirements of what the Church deems binding and the content was not of the nature that God intended. Therefore, when you are granted an annulment, you have the Church's assurance that you are free to marry. This is a much more benevolent approach than those of some other denominations that tend to alienate divorced persons, or even insist they remain unmarried for life.

This simple explanation does not do justice to the intense, highly involved process of annulment. Divorce is not taken lightly in the Catholic Church, and neither is annulment. Procurators and Tribunal members carefully weigh all the evidence and make decisions based on much prayer.

There are other, more personal reasons for you to go through the annulment process. As mentioned before, it can be a tremendous time of healing, forgiveness, and reconciliation for you and your family. As you understand what went wrong in your previous marriage, you can mature and grow spiritually, then be ready to face your new marriage with clearer eyes and more realistic expectations. You can learn to forgive others and forgive yourself, then get on with your life, free from the old baggage of guilt, anger, inconsolable hurt, or bitterness. The person who said that whatever doesn't kill you makes you stronger had a good point. For a purely personal benefit, you can view the entire annulment process as an exercise in self discipline. You can become a stronger and better person because of it.

When you finish, you will have learned so much about yourself, it's practically a private therapy session. You will see the areas in your life where you are weak, and can then lean more heavily on God for wisdom and rely more confidently on God in times of trouble. You will gain better insight into what a good marriage ought to be.

Hopefully, you and your partner will comprehend the nature of a sacramental marriage and be willing to put forth the effort to make it so. In a truly sacramental marriage, both partners will be depending upon God for help. One will not be carrying the burden alone.

If both partners are sincerely searching for solutions, there is nothing that cannot be resolved, healed, or forgiven when you are on your knees before God. "Let us therefore approach the throne of grace with boldness, so that we may receive mercy and find grace to help in time of need" (Hebrews 4:16). When the children of God call out, God is there, offering perfect love and holy power.

As a non-Catholic, you can also consider the annulment process as a sacrifice of true love. After all, you don't *have to* do it. If you choose not to, however, you and your Catholic partner cannot be married with the blessing of the Church, and this can be a negative factor for both of you. In a truly sacramental marriage, you support each other in your spiritual growth, whether or not you agree wholeheartedly with your spouse's denominational differences. You encourage each other in your respective faiths. Whether *you* believe what your partner believes is not nearly as important as the fact that your partner *does*. As an interchurch couple, you have a unique opportunity to show the world the unity of believers in Christ. Faith in Jesus Christ is what makes us all children of God, and baptism is a sign of that unity. You can both build on the unity that is already there.

> In Christ Jesus you are all children of God through faith. As many of you as were baptized into Christ have clothed yourselves with Christ. There is no longer Jew or Greek, there is no longer slave or free, there is no longer male and female; for all of you are one in Christ Jesus.
>
> GALATIANS 3:26-28

Basic differences are integral to certain denominations, so focus on what unites you as a couple and don't let your love starve to death by insisting on gnawing on bones of contention. It is possible to grow in your own faith while supporting the faith of your spouse. Some situations may call for loving solutions, as well as compromise at times, but both of you can continue in your respective faith traditions, in the unity of your basic Christian faith. Live the truth of Galatians 2:20, that the same Christ who loved you and gave himself for you also lives in you right now at this very moment. If you ask, he will give both of you the courage and wisdom to know how to keep your unity in difficult situations.

One woman, having gone through a verbally abusive marriage, was extremely reluctant about going through the annulment process and dredging up painful memories again. When she realized that refusing the annulment would limit her fiancé's participation in the Church, she respected both his conscience and his faith; she decided to do it out of love for him. During her writing of the essays, her fiancé held her when she cried and listened when she sobbed out her frustrations. Reflecting on her pain, he told her later that he realized how much she loved him because no one had ever gone through anything that hard for him. The annulment process confirmed their love and their unity blossomed under the strength of understanding.

As a non-Catholic, deciding to go ahead with an annulment can be a complicated decision. It requires deep thought about sensitive issues. As representatives of the Church, priests and procurators need to walk a fine line between what should be and what, in reality, is. Canon law was given to uphold Church teaching, but a law stands only to underscore a value; it should not be made more important than the needs of people. In ministering to hurting individuals, it is sometimes necessary to look into and pursue other pastoral solutions.

As previously stated, the annulment process itself is exhausting but very rewarding. It is a channel for healing which, although beginning as a legal process, can continue an introspective contemplation that flows out to a life of freedom. As a non-Catholic, your best approach is probably to view the "ordeal" as an act of sacrificial love. In walking through the dark valley of painful memories, you may have to experience a certain amount of emotional death so that your partner can live a fuller spiritual life.

There is no greater love.

PART TWO

———— ✿ ————

HEALING

CHAPTER SIX

Facing Reality

"By the time I was done putting my soul down on paper, the annulment had done its work, as far as I was concerned. I had over fifty pages that chronicled my marriage. I handed the whole package over to the priest and let it go."

"I was told about the sacramental and legal parts, but not about any healing. I didn't know the annulment was supposed to help me that way."

"When I got that letter saying my 'ex' was filing for annulment, I was hurt and upset at first. It was like a slap in the face! I had done what the Church told me to do to try to keep my marriage going, and now they're telling me the last fifteen years were all a waste of time?"

"I was in complete denial about my part in the breakup of my marriage. I didn't have a clue as to what happened until I started answering the annulment questions. My 'ex' and I were both immature and made mistakes."

Working through the annulment process, you are prodded into thinking about what was wrong in your marriage. If you can learn from your mistakes, you will not be prone to repeat them. The annulment helps you face yourself honestly, and accept the reality of what actually happened. If you or your former spouse have the tendency to lay all the blame on each other, insisting you never did anything that could possibly have contributed to the failure of your marriage, then the annulment questions can be mighty thought-provoking.

When answered truthfully, these essay questions force you to take a good long look at reality, and to admit your own part in shaping it. It takes some mighty fancy mental gymnastics to blithely breeze through these searching questions without admitting to at least some contribution to the conflict. Scripture warns against maintaining your own innocence while pointing fingers at others.

> Do not judge, so that you may not be judged. For with the judgment you make you will be judged, and the measure you give will be the measure you get. Why do you see the speck in your neighbor's eye, but do not notice the log in your own eye? Or how can you say to your neighbor, 'Let me take the speck out of your eye,' while the log is in your own eye? You hypocrite, first take the log out of your own eye, and then you will see clearly to take the speck out of your neighbor's eye.
>
> MATTHEW 7:1-5

The annulment process can help you define realistic expectations for marriage and recognize where the breakdown occurred in your previous relationship. New paths can be opened for learning skills in communication, conflict management, or finances. With God's help, you can become aware of how you need to change or the type of partner you need to avoid, as well as the type of partner you need to be.

Through answering the annulment questions, you may, for example, come to understand that even though your spouse was addicted to her career, you "enabled" her to continue that addiction by making excuses to your children, your family, and your friends concerning why she was so often absent. The fact that she spent so much time at work made you seethe in anger and frustration, yet you never confronted her or sought marriage counseling to try to solve the problem. Now that you know you were part of the problem, you can recognize any symptoms that may materialize in the future and be better prepared to avoid repeating those same mistakes. You will no longer be part of the problem. You will be able to work toward a solution in your new relationship.

By assuming responsibility for your own life in the past, you can also gain control of your future. You don't want the same forces of conflict to be present in your next marriage. Blaming your future spouse in the same way you harassed your former spouse can result in another failed marriage.

It's easier to blame others than to admit your faults, either to yourself or to others. Accepting responsibility can be very disturbing. But the growth process really begins when you can come to terms with *your* faults, *your* hurts, *your* feelings, *your* actions, and *your* problems—and you can embrace them *as your own*. A great deal of healing can come through the simple realization that, no matter how hard you may try to be perfect, no one is. That's human nature; it's the reality of living in a sinful world. Sometimes you try to live up to the expectations of others, and then feel guilty when you fail. In the real world, there is no perfect husband or perfect wife. You cannot be the absolute fulfillment of someone else's dreams, nor should you place that impossible burden on the shoulders of your spouse. God is the only one who can ever meet *all* our needs.

"[God's] divine power has given us everything needed for life and godliness, through the knowledge of him who called us by his own glory and goodness" (2 Peter 1:3). True happiness begins when you start looking to God for fulfillment of your needs. Once you realize that people, being imperfect, can never equal the perfect love that God gives, it is easier to let go of that idealistic dream of the "perfect" marriage.

Guilt and regret are released once you understand this. The burden of making someone else happy is unrealistic. You can do good and make another person's life better through God's grace, as Philippians 2:13 teaches, but the choice to be happy is ultimately up to each individual person—including you. Nowhere is it written in the wedding vows that the sole purpose in marriage is to make each other happy.

In a few cases, because of mental illness or an unrepentant heart, the breakdown of your marriage may have been caused, for the most part, by external factors or by your spouse. This will become clear to you as you answer the essay questions honestly. Indeed, you may feel like a failure because you loved someone who didn't love you in return. It will help you to realize that your love could not be returned because of the mental or spiritual state of your spouse. Once you are securely resting in the amazing, eternal love of God, you can begin to let those feelings of worthlessness and despair go and stop berating yourself for being a failure.

If you are experiencing mental anguish, emotional pain, or sorrow, stop to take a good, long look at what God says about you. "But to all who received him, who believed in his name, he gave power to become children of God" (John 1:12). If you are a child of God, you stand as a recipient of an astounding number of blessings. The entire first chapter of Ephesians is full of them—blessed in Christ, chosen in him, adopted through Jesus Christ, redeemed by his blood, forgiven; you are his inheritance, his power is available to you, you are a part of the Church which is his body.

God promises to comfort and guide us; "do not fear, for I am with you, do not be afraid, for I am your God" (Isaiah 41:10). With God's own loving presence in you, you can run to God, weep on God's shoulder. You can give over your aching heart, and ask God to exchange your pain for divine joy. God wants to give you "the oil of gladness instead of mourning, the mantle of praise instead of a faint spirit" (Isaiah 61:3).

Because God is God, exactly as the divine Word says, you must also be the beloved child that God says you are. You can count on these blessings and promises even when you don't understand God's mysterious ways of working, and especially when you don't feel "worthy" to be called a child of God. So clean out the attic of your memories and throw away any mental boxes labeled "if only"—"if only I had...if only he would...if only I hadn't," and all like them. These are useless to you in your emotional healing. You cannot change what has been; you can only work on what will be. Learn from your mistakes, and rely on God's help not to repeat them. "If any of you is lacking in wisdom, ask God" (James 1:5).

In the following chapters, we'll go into more detail and give some examples of how to receive healing in different areas of your life. Remember that it may be a long walk toward freedom from anger, guilt, bitterness, and grief. All in God's time and in God's way.

And you are not alone.

CHAPTER SEVEN

Forgiveness

"The person I needed most to forgive was me. I was so angry with myself for being so insecure that I would allow myself to be treated in such a lousy way! How could I have been so stupid?"

"When I finally made the choice to forgive my former sister-in-law for damaging my reputation with her lies, I felt better immediately. I just don't have any contact with her anymore."

"At first I felt God was to blame for the breakup of my marriage. Why didn't God do something to stop my husband from cheating on me? But I realized that we all have a free will. My husband chose to sin—against me and against God."

"My unforgiving attitude was making me bitter against my ex-wife until I read somewhere that God takes care of injustice. So I mentally placed her in God's hands and let go of my resentment. God will have to deal with her."

The word "forgive" has several meanings in Hebrew and Greek. It carries the meanings of sending forth, letting go, lifting, taking up and away, granting as a favor in kindness, releasing, and setting at liberty. It calls to mind letting a captive bird fly away free and unencumbered, no strings attached. But forgiveness liberates in more than one way. When you forgive others, you are setting yourself free as well.

The key to emotional healing is learning to forgive. At first glance, this sounds simplistic and a bit pious, especially if you are the respondent who isn't seeking an annulment at all. It's easy to blow up in anger at a former spouse who is now setting the wheels in motion for the legal dismissal of your marriage. You'd rather think of revenge than forgiveness.

Today's modern solution is, "Don't get mad—get even." But forgiveness means letting go of your "right" to get even. There really is no way to get even, after all. The damage has already been done, and there is little you can do to make the other person feel your pain or your anger. What empowers you now is your capacity to heal your own past. An unforgiving attitude will choke healing from you, and may have a damaging influence on your children and your future marriage. If you enter into a new marriage with bitterness and unresolved conflicts, you will be dragging a great deal of harmful baggage with you.

This useless baggage is what the annulment process can help you leave behind so that you can get on with your life in a new relationship, free of the underlying problems in the old relationship. The annulment essays can help you to focus on the problems in your previous marriage so that you can see what was missing, what needs were not met, what promises were not kept. You will be better prepared to recognize the symptoms of old problems cropping up—rather like weeds—and be ready to root them out before they can take hold in your new relationship.

A newly married couple was driving to a meeting and happened to miss the turnoff. The husband, who was driving, realized the error at once and commented to his wife that they had missed the exit. The wife, remembering her former marriage, buried her hands in her lap and became very quiet, fearfully awaiting the verbal beating she had always been subjected to by her former spouse. When her husband simply asked her to help him figure out an alternate route to their destination, it slowly dawned on her that he wasn't going to blame her for what had happened, and she began to cry softly. In talking it over later, she told her husband, "It is such a relief to know that I can feel safe with you, that you're not going to blame me for everything and call me filthy names." Now both of them are more aware of how situations can trigger old reactions, and the wife is able to recognize the symptoms and remind herself that she is not still trapped in her old, abusive marriage. She was able to forgive her former husband because she understood his mental state to be unstable. By forgiving, she was free to love again.

Are you despondent because you were abandoned? You may need to forgive your former spouse. Are you angry because you hate being alone? You may need to forgive yourself. Are you feeling bitter because of the Church's policy about annulment? You may need to forgive the Church.

Forgiveness does not mean compliance. It does not mean that what happened is now all right. It's not all right. You've been hurt, emotionally bruised, and you are justifiably angry. Forgiveness does not mean that you will forget the offense, or even be completely free of pain from past memories. Nor does it mean you are condoning wrong or harmful actions. You are not simply acting as if nothing bad had ever happened. True forgiveness is much more powerful, and it requires a good deal of courage on your part.

Forgiveness involves an act of the will that releases your offender from any further action toward you. You expect nothing because nothing else is expected. Forgiveness hands over to God both the offense and the offender. God will vindicate you—maybe in your lifetime, maybe at the final judgment. Maybe you won't see it, but in God's time and in God's way, it will be handled.

You might look at it this way. Say someone owes you money. You could badger him for payment—phoning him, leaving messages for him at work, pounding on his door at midnight—all to no avail. Then you hire a lawyer to garnishee his wages. You get the satisfaction of having your money repaid, and you never even have to face him again. In the same way, forgiveness is letting your Heavenly Lawyer handle your retribution.

In her wonderfully insightful doctoral dissertation, *The Role of Forgiveness in Emotional Healing: A Theological and Psychological Analysis*, Laura Jo Robinson talks about forgiveness as being a lifelong process of practicing the choice to forgive. She defines forgiveness as a gift, neither earned nor deserved, and it involves risk to the one offering it in that the forgiver reaches out to face and understand the offense, and then continues reaching even further toward hope and healing. She cautions that withholding forgiveness puts the offended person in a morally superior position, that it is a self-protective use of power that can hinder the healing process.

Robinson gives five steps involved in the process of forgiveness, which are paraphrased here: 1) accept that you have been injured emotionally; 2) allow yourself time for reflection, to distance yourself emotionally from the incident in order to see clearly what happened (here is where the annulment questions fit in perfectly); 3) decide, as an act of will, that you will forgive; 4) underscore this decision with a positive action, such as showing kindness to your offender, or doing some symbolic act like writing down the offense and then throwing it away; and finally, 5) refuse to continue dwelling on the offense, and gradually your strong feelings of anger or hurt will subside.

In these five steps, the process is a very active one on the part of the person who chooses to forgive. There is a cost to forgiveness because it isn't fair or logical. But it is very powerful. It takes far more courage to forgive than to strike back. When you choose to forgive the wrong done to you, you may remember that you were cruelly hurt, but you will never be destroyed or embittered by the hurt.

Humility is at the core of forgiveness. When you forgive, you also realize your own need of forgiveness from God and from others. When you seek forgiveness, have the same attitude of humility. In other words, it is not enough simply to state in a huff, "Well, I'm sorry if I did anything to hurt you." All that shows is an insensitive mindset of superiority bent on crushing the injured one even further. It lacks an expression of actual repentance. A true and honest request for forgiveness states, "I was wrong. I'm sorry I hurt you. Will you forgive me?" There follows a sincere attempt, through God's grace, to not repeat the offense.

Forgiveness involves a change of heart. It doesn't work to expect or demand forgiveness from others simply because "that's the way Christians are supposed to be." Keep your relationship right with God by removing the log out of your own eye first. God takes care of other people's relationships with their Creator. That is a divine prerogative.

Once you understand the principle behind the cost and

the benefits of forgiveness, you will find that the way of forgiveness is the pathway to healing. Forgiveness is a choice, not an emotion. It does not mean you are condoning any person or action; it is simply letting go of your "right" to revenge. Clinging stubbornly to an unforgiving attitude will chain you to bitterness and anger, and to your past. It can come to the point where you use your anger to avoid dealing honestly with your hurt or grief, and this can build up a preoccupation with the offense. In refusing to release your offender, you are imprisoning yourself as well.

You can forgive others as God has forgiven you because the price for that forgiveness has been paid—"... forgiving one another, as God in Christ has forgiven you" (Ephesians 4:32). You can be healed because the price for your healing has also been paid—"...he was wounded for our transgressions, crushed for our iniquities; upon him was the punishment that made us whole, and by his bruises we are healed" (Isaiah 53:5).

The choice is yours: to forgive or not.

Chapter Eight

Forgiving Others

"My husband left me for another woman, and imagine my shock when I discovered it was my best friend! To this day, I don't have a really close woman friend."

"It's amazing—after I truly forgave my wife, I started praying for her. Well, at least I stopped praying that she'd get run over by a bus!"

"I wasn't the one going after the annulment, so I was pretty ticked off when the Tribunal notified me that my wife was trying to get our marriage annulled. I decided not to answer their questions. I just wanted to forget that entire part of my life. They have no right intruding."

"I was so furious with my priest and the whole annulment process that I didn't enjoy attending Mass anymore. Not only did I have to endure those awful memories all over again, but they expected me to pay for it besides! It wasn't fair!"

When you pray the prayer Jesus taught, you pray for God's will to be done "on earth as it is in heaven." Since there is a need to pray in this way, it's obvious that God's will is *not* being done on earth. What prevents this is that wonderful gift of free will. God created you in the divine image, and because God has a free will to choose, you are made with the ability to choose as well. It is God's hope and desire that you *freely choose* to be in a loving relationship with God.

When you, or your spouse, choose instead to pursue a selfish or demanding path, it can lead to the breakup of a marriage. Unrealistic expectations abound. Instead of getting unconditional love, you get—or give—limited love that is based on performance. In essence, you become debt collectors, checking off each time your spouse fails to live up to your expectations. (One man even kept a file folder on all his wife's "offenses"!) Then you wave this long list in front of each other as evidence that you have not been paid what you are owed. You become disillusioned because your marriage hasn't turned out like you thought it would. Resentment and anger naturally follow.

Through the annulment essays, you may come to realize that you are harboring resentment and anger against someone, most likely your former spouse, which can turn mere hurt feelings into a hardened, bitter spirit. The Holy Spirit may prompt you to make the choice to forgive. Forgiveness is not easy—it costs…often dearly—but it is very powerful.

In his easily readable, down-to-earth book, *A Gentle Thunder, Hearing God Through the Storm*, Max Lucado writes about the difference between the human view of forgiveness and the divine view. The speaker, Logic, argues that the offender doesn't deserve forgiveness. Jesus agrees—and adds that neither does the speaker.

Therein lies the key to forgiving others—not because they deserve your forgiveness but because you realize that you don't deserve God's forgiveness either. Therefore, you can choose to bestow it upon others as freely as God did because of Calvary. When you consider how much it cost the Savior to gain God's forgiveness for you, does it make sense to withhold your forgiveness from one who has wronged you?

The parable of the unforgiving servant in Matthew 18:21-35 warrants careful reading. It doesn't matter how enormous or how trivial the offense. Forgiveness is necessary. Injury of any size punches a hole in the wall of your identity. Forgiveness repairs it.

You may not even have to offer forgiveness directly to the one who hurt you. You can keep this decision strictly between you and God, if you feel so led. One woman used visualization to help her forgive her husband and her best friend for their unfaithfulness. Every time she thought about what they had done, she mentally placed them at the foot of the cross where Jesus was suffering as payment for their sin. In her mind, she backed away and left them there. In this way, she was able to forgive them as she began to understand that they no longer owed her a debt: They owed Jesus.

When you make the choice to forgive another, it is important to understand that forgiveness may *trigger* reconciliation but it does *not* guarantee it. God offers forgiveness to all, but all do not accept it. The same principle applies to your forgiveness of others. Your gracious and generous act of mercy may be met, not with a tearful hug, but with a blank stare. If this happens, leave the final resolution in God's hands. When you offer forgiveness and it is refused, you are still free; it is the unforgiving one who remains chained. *Forgiveness does not change the offender; it changes you.*

In choosing to forgive others, you meet another costly choice: Will you let your past memories continue to control you, or will you allow God's peace to guide you in the future? Letting go of the hurt and anger also means letting go of the memory. This doesn't mean you will never again remember what happened. It means you will remember it in a different light, so that it won't have the power to overwhelm you again. But you will need to develop a new mental pattern, a new way of dealing with the old memories.

First, you decide not to dwell on any situation you have chosen to forgive. This is not the same as denial. You are not denying what happened. You have already carefully studied the situation through the annulment essays, analyzed it, and faced your own responsibility for its occurrence; you have already made the choice to forgive the other involved party. Stewing, fretting, and mulling over the offense constantly is harmful to your emotional well-being. In forgiving, you also use your free will to set aside bad thoughts that are counterproductive to healing.

Second, you replace the bad thoughts with good ones. As the old saying goes, "You can't stop the birds from flying over your head, but you can keep them from building a nest in your hair." So when the old memories come back to haunt you, shoo them away with new thoughts. God's Word teaches you to let your mind meditate on the good.

> Finally, beloved, whatever is true, whatever is honorable, whatever is just, whatever is pure, whatever is pleasing, whatever is commendable, if there is any excellence and if there is anything worthy of praise, think about these things.
>
> PHILIPPIANS 4:8

When ugly thoughts invade your mind, crowd them out with pleasant memories of better times: of that friend who has always supported you, of the loving faces of your family, of your favorite vacation spot by the lake, of your future mate, of all God's blessings. When you develop an attitude of thankfulness, you begin to see divine mysterious workings on your behalf, and you find it easier to reach out for God's comfort.

The marvel of the human mind is that you can be in the past, present, and imaginative future in a matter of seconds. Learn to distract yourself: You can *choose* what you want to think. It may sound trite, but it works. Use your free will to change your mind about how you remember your past. They are only memories; they don't have to devastate you any longer.

Talking with and spilling out your emotions to a loving God can be very healing. The closer you get to God's heart, the more you understand how safe you are in God's care. You can yell and scream, letting all your latent frustrations out, and God will not admonish you. God comprehends completely the entire situation, from beginning to end, all the time loving you. Remember, God knows you through and through. The very hairs of your head are counted. You are greatly loved.

It may help to do something symbolic to further cement the act of forgiveness in your mind. One man took a roll of toilet paper and wrote down his anger against his former wife and relatives. When he was finished, he flushed it. He felt a great sense of release as he watched the paper swirl out of sight. One woman took a legal pad and wrote down all the abusive things her former husband had done and said. Then she took a red marker and drew a line through each item, signifying that this was now forgiven and under the blood of Jesus. She crumpled the paper, threw it away, and never again let her mind dwell on what she had written. Another woman mentally placed her anger and hurt in the packet that contained her finished annulment papers. When she handed it to her priest, in her mind, she let the harmful emotions go too. You can release balloons, capture fireflies and set them free— anything your imagination can come up with—to help you symbolize your freedom through forgiveness.

Do something humorous, if that's your style. Humor puts an entirely different perspective on things, and can give hope in what appears to be a hopeless situation. Write the name of your divorce lawyer on a baseball and hit it out of the park! Use a soda can as a microphone and sing the blues. As your mother used to say, "Consider this just another character-building experience," and think of what a character you've become! The next time you crack open a peanut, look at the empty shell and compare it to your divorce: this is only the shell; the nut is gone! When faced with a particularly difficult essay question in the annulment papers, think of your favorite comedy stars and imagine how they might answer it. Of course, don't write down your imaginings as your answer! Just enjoy a good chuckle, then get back to work.

In answering the annulment questions, you may discover that you have unresolved conflicts, stemming from childhood or adolescence, that have influenced the breakup of your marriage, or you may feel a particular person or situation impossible to forgive. You may need professional counseling in order to resolve the conflicts in your own mind, so that you can forgive the past and reach out toward a hopeful future. There are Christian therapists, psychologists, and counselors who are qualified to give you the guidance you need. But be aware of the hazard of getting "stuck" in therapy. You can be helped, but there is also the possibility that you can become overly preoccupied with your own healing, enjoying the attention rather than really wanting to get well.

Jesus understood this principle when he asked the sick man at the pool of Bethesda, "Do you want to be made well?" (John 5:6). If you truly want to be made well, you must be willing to do what God tells you is necessary for your healing. That may include forgiving, and forgiving is a difficult thing to do. But God is always willing to help us learn to forgive.

Corrie Ten Boom wrote about her experience at the hands of the Nazis in her book, *The Hiding Place*. Many years later, during a lecture tour, she recognized a man in the audience as a former Gestapo guard at the concentration camp where her beloved sister had died. When he came up to shake her hand, she at first was repulsed. Mentally struggling, Corrie came to understand that if she couldn't forgive this man, then all she had said that night about God's love was a lie. Inwardly, Corrie prayed fervently for God's own forgiveness to flow through her— out to this man—because she couldn't forgive him on her own. And she was able to take his hand in the spirit and the love of Christ, for his sake and for what he had done for her at Calvary. When something is too heavy for you to lift, ask for help in carrying it.

This principle is the same in spiritual matters. When you confront something too hard for you, ask for help from the God who loves you and is waiting to come to your aid with all the forces of heaven. Ask God for healing. Seek it earnestly, knowing that you, having once been wounded, will make a better guide for others who have also been wounded. Resting in God's love and relying on God's strength will make you more like Christ. Being healed will make you more sensitive to the needs of others and shield your soul from the anger that leads to bitterness.

Bitter anger builds walls; it blinds you from seeing the truth. The grip of rage can deceive you into thinking you don't really need God—you can handle things just fine on your own. Your faith in God will be stunted as long as you refuse God's healing touch. To truly set you free, God needs entry into every part of your life. This includes your past. Independence from God's love will not lead you into healing.

Bitter anger clutched in self-righteousness will not lead to healing either, because it doesn't allow forgiveness. Holding on to past hurts is a decision to suffer unnecessarily. Bitter anger stews and bubbles; it recounts old injuries, licking past wounds so that they become infected, never able to heal.

Anger doesn't have to degenerate into bitterness. Anger, after all, is a legitimate, God-given emotion; it is okay to be angry. The sin is not in feeling the anger itself, but rather in any wrongful actions that might accompany your anger, or in refusing God's comfort by hanging on to your anger instead of letting yourself be healed. This is not what God intended when gifting you with the emotion of anger. "Be angry but do not sin; do not let the sun go down on your anger, and do not make room for the devil" (Ephesians 4:26-27).

Anger can be very protective, in a positive sense, if you transfer the rage onto the situation rather than the person. It's like loving the sinner while hating the sin. Consider the battered wife who is divorced by her abusive husband. Over time, she regains her self-esteem and realizes her worth as a human being. When she is ready to begin dating again, her righteous anger at having been beaten can protect her from entering another abusive relationship.

One woman put it this way: "If I learned one thing from the divorce, it was not to back down when being treated unfairly. No one is ever going to speak to me that way again. I won't let it happen." Her God-given anger will protect her from abuse.

The rage a parent feels over losing a child in a drunk driving accident can change legislation, start up organizations, and begin programs to warn people of the dangers of driving drunk. In cases such as these, anger is a motivating force for positive change, a constructive rather than destructive action. Anger can help you or hurt you. Be sure you know what kind of anger is motivating you before you begin walking the path to emotional healing.

One of the best books on emotional healing is *Healing Life's Hurts: Healing Memories Through Five Stages of Forgiveness*, by Matthew and Dennis Linn. Chapter Twelve is an excellent example of how Christ can heal through the Eucharist and a willing heart. The authors advocate that true healing comes when you can finally thank God for your painful memories because you can see how you have grown through your pain and become a better person because of it. Thanking God for the growth that hurts is indeed a big step.

As tough as it is to admit, you must also face the fact that it is possible you may not be completely healed of your painful past. In the Hebrew Scriptures, Jacob was not healed of the wound he received while wrestling with the angel. In the New Testament, Paul was not healed of the affliction he called "a thorn" in his flesh.

These saints probably did not comprehend all of God's ways, but Paul was able to conclude that God could turn anything, no matter how bad, into something beneficial (see Romans 8:28). Even though you don't understand all of God's workings, through faith you can come to accept them, even welcome them as gifts from a loving God. Especially if you have to interact with your former spouse because of joint custody of the children, you will need God's grace to handle each situation with dignity. Forgiveness may have to come frequently. And you may never be completely free of your emotional burden, but through the strength of Christ, you won't be crushed by it.

Perhaps you need to forgive someone in your church— God, your priest, or even the Church itself. Think through your emotions and find the root cause of your feelings. Maybe what you need is reconciliation with God, or perhaps acceptance of God's mysterious workings on your behalf. If you are angry with God, say so. It is safe to cry out to God in frustration and despair, as Jonah, Jeremiah, and Elijah did. God knows your true thoughts and understands human nature. God will hold you steady, soothing you, rocking you quietly, as if you were a sobbing child on your mother's lap. Longing to know God's great love and wisdom better, you will grow in faith and in spiritual knowledge. You can never fully understand God in this life, but you can learn to love God better, and to rest in the unfathomable love that God has for you.

You can vent all your frustrations in prayer, knowing that the Spirit will filter out whatever is inappropriate so that the true intention of your heart comes up before God. The Spirit knows your needs better than you do.

> Likewise the Spirit helps us in our weakness; for we do not know how to pray as we ought, but that very Spirit intercedes with sighs too deep for words. And God, who searches the heart, knows what is the mind of the Spirit, because the Spirit intercedes for the saints according to the will of God.
>
> ROMANS 8:26-27

Recall the now-famous poem, *Footprints*, in which a person rethinks his life as if he were walking along a beach with God. During the most painful times in his life, he sees only one set of footprints left in the sand, and questions God: Why did you abandon me in my times of need? God gently reassures the person: God loves him, and where there is only one set of footprints, God carried him. God is ever present in your pain and your suffering; you just need to be reminded of it sometimes.

You may want to pray that God will make the divine presence known to you, that your eyes will be opened to God's loving care. You are God's beloved child. When you hurt, God hurts. When you feel abandoned, God is always there, ready to wrap you in the security of divine protection. When you are emotionally betrayed and wronged, God is already preparing your vindication.

You may feel that your procurator or your priest has been unsympathetic. Perhaps you have even felt alienated from the congregation because of your divorce. Remember, no one who has not gone through a divorce can ever truly understand your situation or the emotional upheaval brought about by an annulment. Those in the Church who have hurt you most likely have done so out of ignorance; they cannot possibly comprehend your pain. God is the only one who completely understands.

In *Healing Spiritual Abuse*, author Ken Blue makes the interesting point that Jesus saw the multitudes as sheep milling around aimlessly without a shepherd. These people were good synagogue attenders who listened to what their spiritual leaders told them. The scribes and Pharisees were masters of the law of Moses. The problem was, the spiritual leaders obeyed the letter of the law while ignoring the spirit of the law, which was love for God and others. In keeping strict tabs on the people, the scribes and Pharisees overlooked the greater law of mercy and compassion. Although this is not the intention of the Church, some priests and church leaders may have the tendency to abide by canon law alone, letting rules and regulations overshadow the deeper needs of people who are hurting.

One woman left the Church because a nun she had confided in about her pending divorce suddenly became bluntly indifferent. One man harbored resentment against the priest who refused to baptize his severely mentally challenged infant brother. Another woman confessed, "It really threw me when the people of my parish applauded a priest and nun who revoked their vows to get married and yet shunned me because of my divorce. Why was it easier for them to get out of their vows than it was for me?"

These are instances where people reached out for help and others in the Church failed to minister to them. If you, like these people, have felt rejected or ignored in your time of need, you are not alone. Church sanctuaries everywhere are filled with the walking wounded. God's people are still living under the influence of a sinful world. None of us has reached that heavenly perfection yet.

This is not an excuse to treat others with less than loving honor and dignity, but rather a reminder that all people carry burdens of their own. Some are bound by rules and regulations, some carry hidden pain every bit as piercing as yours. Those who did not help you, in all likelihood, could not. Knowing this may make it less difficult for you to forgive them.

Like many people, you may find the prospect of writing down your innermost thoughts in great detail for the scrutiny of strangers a formidable task indeed. Like them, you may be understandably reluctant to begin the annulment process, and may even be looking for a way to avoid it entirely. The annulment fee is often used as this way of avoidance. Each annulment costs around one thousand dollars to process from beginning to end, although this may vary. Individual dioceses suggest a portion of this cost as a fee which is requested—not required—of those petitioning for an annulment, in order to help underwrite some of the costs. The money does not go to the tribunal office, but rather to the local diocese, where it is apportioned as needed.

The annulment fee—or donation, if you will—is based on the premise that the annulment has more "value" if you invest your money in it. This gives you a sense of ownership; you don't feel like a welfare case. Because the requested fee is also based on ability to pay, however, the fee may be waived altogether. In essence, the annulment is free if you are strapped financially. But if the petitioner is able to contribute, then paying a portion of the costs for the annulment is a reasonable appeal to dignity and integrity.

For Catholics and non-Catholics alike, the necessity of annulment has been a source of animosity for years. For most Catholics, the annulment is usually set forth (first) as a requirement of canon law in order to stay in good standing with the Church, and (second) as a means of reconciliation with yourself and others. It is primarily a grudgingly accepted legal process.

For non-Catholics, the annulment process might be viewed with much more skepticism: as a means of imposing authority, and therefore an offense that requires forgiveness. It is difficult to consider the annulment as a requirement of canon law rather than as an act of control. Anger and resentment are perfectly natural reactions to what is deemed a required invasion of privacy. Granted, this has been the objection of numerous Catholics as well. How is the conflict resolved, so that the offended party avoids falling into the trap of bitter resentment? By choosing to forgive as God has forgiven, for the sake of Christ. No, it isn't fair, and it won't give the satisfaction of revenge, but it is a powerful tool for building personal healing and spiritual growth.

The Catholic Church and its Tribunal do not desire to "torture" you by making you go through an annulment. It is absolutely essential, according to canon law, in order to determine whether or not you are truly free to marry. If you wish to remain a practicing Catholic under the full blessing of the Church, or if you wish to marry a practicing Catholic who wishes to remain under the full blessing of the Church, it is necessary.

You cannot change the fact of the annulment. What you can do is pray. Ask God to change your heart and your attitude, and, if you need this extra step, to help you forgive the Church for making you go through this painful necessity. Forgiveness costs, but if you remain full of anger against the Church, try weighing the cost of non-forgiveness. It costs you little to forgive the Church; you probably won't even have to speak to anyone but God. Refusing to forgive may cost you your next marriage. You will be nursing a grudge, fueling a fire of resentment that will eventually make you a person with a bitter spirit, difficult to live with and impossible to please.

Is it worth that? Isn't a life of freedom in Christ far better?

CHAPTER NINE

Forgiving Yourself

"She was pregnant and it was my fault. I thought I had to marry her. We were too young and the marriage was awful. After the divorce, I felt like I'd ruined three lives."

"I hate myself for being so weak, but I don't want to be alone. I thought getting married in the Catholic Church would mean I'd always have someone. Now I feel like such a failure."

"How could I have been so blind? I should have known from the way he treated all women that he wouldn't treat me any better. My friends warned me, but I didn't listen."

"At first, I blamed my ex-wife for divorcing me, but now I see how my macho attitude destroyed our marriage. I wish I could go back and undo everything. I was just so stupid."

Honestly evaluating yourself can be very painful. Realizing your own mistakes can lead to deeply felt feelings of guilt and remorse. You don't have to feel trapped by these feelings. God is able to cleanse even a guilty conscience.

Many times, past guilt is simply a "learned" behavior: an attitude that has been laid on you by well-meaning friends, a strict religious setting, or even your own parents. This kind of guilt is best if recognized and set aside. It has no place in true inner emotional healing. Actual, beneficial guilt, on the other hand, builds conscience and character by allowing you to look at your problems through the viewpoint of others, thereby keeping their concerns on the same level as your own. The Holy Spirit may be nudging your conscience, out of your need to make something right or ask someone's forgiveness, in order to alleviate your real guilt.

Through prayer, and perhaps the advice of someone you trust, you can discern whether the guilt you feel is of the positive or negative variety. If you discern your guilt to be the "learned" (negative) kind, you may be needlessly punishing yourself for something that happened in the past which was not your fault. If this is the case, you need to pray to be freed from the "sense" of guilt. Hearing a priest's absolution can be a great relief, but if even this does not bring peace to your heart, there is no shame in seeking professional guidance.

In answering the annulment questions, you may come to realize that the one you most need to forgive is yourself. The process starts out the same as forgiving others: Carefully examine what has happened in a realistic light, accept your responsibility and "own" your own problems without blaming anyone else, then choose to let it go; and forgive yourself as God forgives, because Christ has paid the price for your freedom.

However, there are some important differences when it comes to forgiving yourself. There may be the necessity of restitution on your part for something you have done to someone else. If your conscience is bothering you over the divorce settlement, for example, do your best to make it right before God. Ignoring the necessity of restitution will not make it go away. Write those letters of apology, return those items, divide up that money, ask forgiveness of your former spouse. Do whatever you feel the Holy Spirit is prompting you to do in order to clear your conscience.

Another difference is the aspect of asking God's forgiveness first, before you bestow forgiveness upon yourself. In fact, you may feel it impossible to forgive yourself before you know God's forgiveness. Depending on your faith, and the severity of what you need forgiveness for, this may come only through a time of prayer and humility before God's holiness as you honestly seek mercy. You may want to pray with someone you trust, such as your priest or a close friend. It can be a great relief to hear someone else agree that God has indeed forgiven you. This is one of the reasons why the sacrament of reconciliation is so highly beneficial.

Probably the most important difference, though, is that forgiving yourself can be more difficult than forgiving others because you don't feel worthy of God's forgiveness. Through writing the annulment essays, your mistakes may seem to loom larger than life and you may feel overwhelmed with remorse. You may feel that what you've done is so "bad" you're not even worth God's time, and surely God will not "waste" precious time with you. Here, amazingly, is where true healing can really begin: when you finally let go of your own self-righteousness and see yourself bankrupt, as you truly are, and in desperate need of God's loving mercy and powerful grace. When you can at last accept your need to change, and acknowledge that you cannot accomplish this on your own, God can begin to do marvelous work in you.

Turning to God for guidance, and asking reassurance of God's love, is a hard step to take when you're feeling like dirt under someone's feet. Divorce can strip you of your esteem, your confidence, and even your sense of humor. You feel as if the rug has been pulled out from under you, and it takes some time to regain your balance. Immersing yourself in the sacred Scriptures can help your balance. There you can read and see for yourself what God says about you. It can change your attitude; it can change your entire life.

"But to all who received him, who believed in his name, he gave power to become children of God" (John 1:12), and nothing "will be able to separate us from the love of God in Christ Jesus our Lord" (Romans 8:38-39)—not even our own feelings of inadequacy. God "has rescued us from the power of darkness and transferred us into the kingdom of his beloved Son, in whom we have redemption, the forgiveness of sins" (Colossians 1:13-14). "God's Spirit dwells in [us]" (1 Corinthians 3:16) in order "that we may understand the gifts bestowed on us by God" (1 Corinthians 2:12). We have been given new and abundant life (see 2 Corinthians 5:17; John 10:10), and are empowered to do good (see Ephesians 2:10), because "it is no longer [we] who live, but it is Christ who lives in [us]" (Galatians 2:20). And someday we will share in the heavenly glory (see John 14:1-3). Thinking on these wonderful truths can set your spirit soaring high and replace those negative thoughts with praise!

If you are feeling that you don't deserve God's forgiveness—and therefore cannot forgive yourself—consider that *no one* merits God's blessings because *no one* is good enough (Romans 3:23). God offers such wondrous salvation as a gift of grace (Ephesians 2:8-9), just as God freely extends unconditional love (1 John 4:9-10). You can do nothing to "earn" God's acceptance; if you trust in God, you already have it. Meditating on such gracious and inexplicable love for you can protect you from those feelings of unworthiness.

Perhaps you are afraid that what you have done is unforgivable. Jesus invites you to come to him (John 6:37). "If [you] confess [your] sins, he who is faithful and just will forgive [you]…and cleanse [you] from all unrighteousness" (1 John 1:9). God's power and grace can cleanse even your conscience (Hebrews 9:11-14) and set you free (John 8:36). Realize that Christ had to give his perfect life in order to usher in God's forgiveness for you. You may not feel worthy of forgiveness, but God counted you worthy. You are of great value to God, who loves you everlastingly.

If you have asked forgiveness and made the restitution needed, and yet still don't feel forgiven, consider that God understands your heart (1 John 3:18-20) and can see the entire picture from the standpoint of eternity. God knows your true intentions—knows that you have tried to make things as right as you honestly can.

If your guilt and self-beratement are still so great that they overshadow the truths about God's forgiveness, and God's love and concern for you, then do one thing more—and this is another tough decision. Put your feelings and your negative emotions aside, and deal with your free will—that part of you that was also created in God's image. Trust that what God says is true—and *choose to believe* you have been forgiven, whether you feel like it or not. Remember, forgiveness is *not* an emotion: It is a choice—whether you are forgiving yourself or someone else.

After you have chosen to believe that God has forgiven you, refuse to dwell on the matter again. Don't keep digging up what God has buried. Leave the past behind, as Paul did in Philippians 3:13-14, and live the rest of your life for God. Resolve to learn from your mistakes, not remain spiritually paralyzed by them.

Once you have accepted God's forgiveness, it is much easier to forgive yourself. Knowing that God accepts you, warts and all, can be a wonderfully liberating experience. Acceptance from God differs greatly from acceptance from others. Human love, for the most part, is based on what you do; God's love depends solely on who God is. God does not calculate your worth on the basis of either your goodness or your sin. This great love depends solely on God's own faithfulness, and *not* your efforts to "earn" it. There is nothing you can do to change the fact that God *is* love. God continues to love you in spite of your weaknesses and faults.

When you can truly comprehend that God loves and accepts you, then you can learn to love yourself. It is only when you love yourself as God intended that you can reach out to love others in healthy relationships. How can you fulfill God's command to love your neighbor as you love yourself, if you don't love yourself at all? Can you see how a healthy self-love is necessary in order to live the Christian life successfully?

Suppose you have asked God's forgiveness, have forgiven yourself, and now—for the purpose of restitution—you need to ask forgiveness from someone you have hurt deeply.

It may be that person will refuse to forgive you. What do you do then? You have tried to reconcile, you have tried to live at peace with this person (Romans 12:18). You have, in fact, done all that you can do. The rest depends on the offended party. You must leave this in God's hands, let God sort it out. Through God's grace, continue to show love and concern for the one you have injured, and do your best not to repeat your past mistakes. Let it go. God is in control now. There is nothing further you can do.

The use of your God-given imagination can further your healing, if you choose to try this. Picture yourself at Calvary, kneeling at the cross of Christ. For those of you who have done the Stations of the Cross during Lent, this will come easily. Look up at the face of Jesus, and see him suffering and dying for you. Open your heart and your mind to comprehend what it cost him to gain forgiveness for you. Ask him to forgive you, and listen to his gentle voice telling you that he loves you and does indeed forgive you. Let his quiet peace flood over you— melting away your sorrow, your guilt, your fear, and even your self-reproach.

Let the scene change to a few days later at the garden tomb. The heavy stone in the doorway has been rolled away, and a soft, glowing light emanates from inside. Hear the shimmering angel speak the ancient words, "He is not here; he is risen." God has accepted the perfect sacrifice of the "only begotten Son of God," and has proved it to the world by raising Jesus back to life—forever! Because Christ lives, you also have the promise of eternal life through him whom you trust for salvation (Romans 8:11).

This is what your Lord has done *for you*. Through his suffering, death, and resurrection, you can have peace with God (Romans 4:25; 5:1). Jesus holds out his arms, beckoning you to come to him and longing to be your friend—for that is what he says he is. Run to him with joy, laughing like a cherished child of his heart—for that is what he says you are.

CHAPTER TEN

Closure

"It was like tearing my heart out and putting it on paper, but when it was all over, I felt better."

"The annulment questions were tough. They brought up stuff I didn't want to think about, but I had to face the fact that deep down I knew she was never committed to the marriage. I never really had a wife. I cried for weeks."

"Putting all those memories into words was one of the toughest things I've ever done, but now I know I'm in tune with the Church and it will be okay."

"When I gave my finished annulment papers to my priest, it was like releasing a ghost. I could let my 'ex' go."

Writing out the annulment essays can be healing for many reasons, but one of the biggest ones is that of being able to come to closure with your divorce and your former marriage. You can finally end the relationship as husband and wife, and close the door on the existence you knew before. What lies ahead of you is a new frontier, a fresh beginning. You can start over.

The best part of starting over is the knowledge you've gained by carefully and thoroughly answering the essay questions. Now you can know what was wrong in your former marriage, and you can avoid making the same mistakes twice. You can know what you need to do to make your next marriage truly sacramental in nature. You can be on the lookout for problem areas, and know enough to get the help you need as a family *before* trouble erodes your marriage beyond repair. You can become more sensitive to others, more responsive to their needs, more open to their opinions.

In letting your former spouse go, you can grieve over the death of the relationship. You can shed tears over what could have been, and then resolve to utilize your new-found knowledge to allow your next marriage to abound in the loving and graced relationship that God intended. Now you can understand that only God can ever fulfill all your needs. People ultimately fail you because everyone still struggles with sin and is in need of grace and for-giveness. Now your sadness at not having your dreams or ideals met does not have to lead to anger or remorse because you know that nobody is perfect, including yourself.

Working through the grief process into closure takes time. It can take months...or years. You may want to do something concrete to help you finalize this closure. One woman attended a Mass and, after the service, she took up a tiny basket in which she had placed her wedding ring. She left the basket on the altar. It was her way of symbolizing the death of her marriage and the giving of her future into God's hands.

After your divorce, you may have experienced feelings of bewildered displacement. Who are you now, if not a wife or a husband? The annulment can resolve your inner conflict by allowing you to see how you have grown as a person on your own.

You may have suffered verbal, mental, or even physical abuse, been betrayed by an unfaithful spouse, or waited up many nights alone, listening for the key to turn in the lock. Then you went before the divorce court and heard the judge declare your marriage dissolved. It may have been a relief, or it may have been a nightmare—but then you were on your own. Perhaps you handled both a job and childcare, or fixed that leaky faucet, or landed that contract. You faced hardships alone. *And you made it.* You are a stronger person for what you have been through. You understand better what someone else feels when going through a divorce because you have been there. You can empathize and you can help others. That is growth.

You have the right to read the annulment essays written by your former spouse. If you exercise this right, do so with an open mind. Remember that every problem and situation always has at least two sides, and your side will probably not be evident in your former spouse's writings. Reading your former spouse's essays could make you furious, but if you read with an attitude of self-righteous anger, you won't learn a thing. Anger will slow your healing considerably; however, calmly reading another opinion can greatly aid your understanding of what happened in the marriage.

If you choose to let your future spouse read your annulment essays, it could open avenues of discussion on touchy subjects such as finances, sex, marriage roles, tempers, or in-laws. Not only can the annulment close the door on your past, it can open the door to communication for your future as well. Numerous misunderstandings occur when one partner is left in the dark, but when you can openly discuss potential problem areas, the chances are better for a successful marriage. One man was too embarrassed to admit his insecurity, but when his fiancée read his annulment essays, she came to see his deep longing for intimacy, which was overlooked in his first marriage. Consequently, she goes out of her way to tell him of her love daily, packing notes in his sack lunch, playing his favorite music, even buying special greeting cards.

Although writing out the essay questions can self-minister, you may choose to do something else positive or creative to alleviate your grief and bring it to closure. Missionary Elisabeth Elliot brought good out of her grief when she returned to the Auca Indians in Ecuador who had murdered her husband. So moved were the Aucas by her life of love and forgiveness that they turned their hearts to God. When C. S. Lewis lost his beloved wife to cancer, he wrote *A Grief Observed* to help him get back on speaking terms with God. The beautiful hymn *O Love That Wilt Not Let Me Go* was written by George Matheson when his fiancée left him because he was going blind. He turned to God in his grief, and now this uplifting song is a blessing to many.

On a personal note, as we ourselves were going through the annulment process, we met many hurting people whose past distressing experiences had been brought out clearly through the annulment essays. Faced with those painful memories, they didn't know how to go beyond them into healing. We saw a great need, and wrote this book as a way of ministering to others. It is our sincere hope that you will also be led to help and comfort others, in your own way, in bringing to closure your past marriage. Give yourself time to grieve, and seek the comfort of God. Set your mind and your heart to believe what Christ says about you—that you are God's beloved child—and allow God to love you.

Galatians 4:6 says that you can call God your Father. The word "abba" carries with it a sense of the familiar—

rather more like "daddy" than "father." Can you imagine yourself relaxing in the arms of God, as a dearly loved child who has fallen and hurt him or herself climbs up into Daddy's lap for comfort?

Moses told the people of Israel: "It was not because you were more numerous than any other people that the LORD set his heart on you and chose you....It was because the LORD loved you" (Deuteronomy 7:7,8). That's it! God loves you…just because God loves you. Rest in that love. It will never change. Even if you strike out at bat, even if you fall off your bicycle, even if your marriage fails, even if you feel no one cares about you anymore, you can always come to your heavenly *Abba*, who loves you just because he loves you.

The conflicts of the past can never be undone, but they don't have to condemn you to a future of failure. Take hope that, with God's grace, past conflicts and painful memories can be victoriously lived with, even if complete healing never takes place. True healing begins when you choose God's joy and freedom over the burden of carrying past mistakes. Healing continues when you attempt reconciliation by learning the choice of forgiveness, when you reach out in love to help others and in so doing work through your own grief, and when you can finally become grateful for what happened in the past as you see yourself growing in grace.

CHAPTER ELEVEN

Dealing with Your Children

"The annulment took a heavy toll on my family. Fortunately, my kids were older, and able to deal with their mom being such an emotional wreck!"

"My son offered to be a witness, and at first I thought that was good. Now I'm wondering how this is going to affect his own marriage. He's still very angry with his dad."

"Ever since the divorce, my little daughter has been so quiet. She won't talk to me about what happened, but I know she must miss her mother. Is it possible for a five-year-old to be depressed?"

"I don't know what to do about my kids. They're disruptive in school, and they've taken to shouting at each other for no reason at all. It's so unlike them to be rebellious. I'm thinking of taking them with me to counseling, but it seems kind of extreme. I mean, they are just kids."

When adults are dealing with a highly charged, emotional period in their lives, often it is their children who are inadvertently overlooked. It is absolutely essential that healing for the children be addressed in these instances as well. Children cannot see their parents going through times of great pain without becoming involved themselves. Unresolved family problems can affect children in numerous ways, and even affect subsequent relationships.

Since most children cannot avoid unhealthy family situations by jumping in the car and driving away or moving out, they tend to escape these conflicts in their own ways. They may become withdrawn and stay in their rooms; they may act out at home or in school; they may transform into "the good child" in an effort to ease tensions; or they may become overly attached to a certain item like a blanket or toy. They may even reveal their stress by bed-wetting or reverting to babyish behavior. Underneath these actions, children hide deep-seated emotions of anger, fear, resentment, and incredible sadness.

In answering the annulment questions, you will have come to a greater understanding of what happened in your previous marriage to cause its breakup. You will have seen where the fault lines were drawn, the shaky foundation on which you and your former spouse attempted unsuccessfully to build. Perhaps you will also have detected patterns of dysfunction or abuse that were allowed to continue from childhood into adulthood and then proceeded to infiltrate your marriage, making it impossible for you and your former spouse to fulfill the requirements for the binding contract called for in Christian marriage. Now would be a good time to start praying about when and how to share this knowledge with your children. Even though it may be painful, it is the loving thing to do. Your children need you. They look to you for guidance, and they follow your example. They deserve at least some of the understanding you have gleaned from the annulment questions.

They may also have questions of their own that require careful answering. Younger children tend to blame themselves for the breakup of a marriage, and they need to know they were not to blame. Older children may be mature enough to understand what went wrong, and why. They need this information, not only to be able to forgive and to deal with their own anger and resentment, but also, hopefully, to avoid falling into the same situations their parents did. It has been well researched and documented that abuse, for example, tends to be perpetuated from one generation to another. The abused can become the abuser. In giving abused children the tools by which to heal and forgive, they may avoid the tragic abuse cycle when the occasion comes for them to marry.

Your honesty may assist them in their future happiness by providing information that will culminate in good choices. Your children have watched how you deal with life, and quite possibly will mirror you in their own dealings. Just as an example, if they are used to living with an alcoholic parent, they may choose to marry an alcoholic spouse because they know how to relate and react to that particular life style; the relationship is familiar. In cases like these, especially, you must lovingly reach out to your children and help them heal, even as you yourself are healing. With God's strength, this is your opportunity to help break the cycle for your children and grandchildren.

This is also an excellent time to instruct your children in their faith. It is, of course, ideal for both parents to contribute to sincere and honest teaching out of love for the children. In reality, however, this is not usually the norm. In cases of abandonment or abuse, where the children have the anchor of only one parent, their healing and reconciliation can still be worked out through the remaining parent. You can teach them about the sacrament of matrimony, and what it takes to have a binding marriage, because the annulment process will have revealed the elements that were missing from your previous marriage. It is also wise to help them see the difference between civil divorce and Church annulment, so they do not come to look at this as a "Catholic divorce." Through your own understanding, you can assure them that they are still your children in every sense of the word. The civil law may have dissolved your marriage, but you and your children are still family, and your former spouse is still their parent in all legitimacy.

If answering the annulment questions was particularly tough, your children may wonder why the Church required this of you. In your own words, depending upon the age and understanding of each child, you might explain that the annulment taught you how to have a better marriage in the future. It showed you many things that could go wrong when two people decide to marry.

When honest people truly want healing, the annulment can be a serviceable tool. When you acknowledge your limitations as a human being, and bring them into the presence of God, your conflicts and struggles can become the enlightenment that draws you toward reconciliation with God, yourself, and others. Your children who are now adults will also benefit from understanding these principles, because they deserve to have their own opportunity for healing and reconciliation with their parents. This is especially true if your adult children were called upon as witnesses for the annulment.

You, your procurator, a priest, or someone from the church should be available to guide the children through their pain and into personal healing. Family counseling is highly recommended. With compassionate therapy, your entire family can grow in empathy for each other, becoming more like Christ, our great example of love and forgiveness. When and how you go about this process of healing will depend greatly on the age and makeup of each individual child. It is recommended that you begin helping your children when you yourself are reconciled with the situation. Then you can talk peacefully about your former marriage and spouse, and be better able to deal with each child's own anger, frustrations, and hurt. It is not necessary that you tell your children every detail of past sins and shortcomings. It may surprise you to discover how much they already know. Discuss honestly and briefly, answer their questions carefully, admit regret for your own contribution to the breakdown of the marriage, and try to explain simply your former spouse's behavior.

No matter how difficult this may be for you, it is essential to describe your former spouse's nature gently but accurately, neither condoning nor condemning. He or she was neither an absolute saint nor a complete villain. Again, separate the sin from the sinner, the situation from the person. It is very important to show this balance in the children's eyes. Your former spouse is still their parent or caregiver. You can help your children heal better if you gently steer them away from feelings of hatred and vengeance. You are teaching them that forgiveness, after all, is giving up your "right" to get even and leaving your vindication and vengeance up to God.

Before your children can forgive, however, they may need to have some safe ways to release pent-up anger, just as you may need to. One boy took a plastic baseball bat to some discarded sofa cushions and beat the stuffing out of them. During therapy sessions, one counselor brought out a toy pop-up clown, weighted with sand, and invited his clients to sock away. Thick boxing gloves, playing tag, or an exhausting game of basketball may fill the ticket. One little girl would jump outside on her trampoline and scream at the top of her lungs.

These are just a few suggestions for ways of coping with intense feelings of rage. Once the rage is out and acknowledged, it is easier to talk about anger and hurt, and then to let it go in a safe way.

Pray with your children. Let them know that they are not alone, that God loves them and cares how they feel, that God will hear them when they cry and comfort them. They can tell God anything; God will understand, and accept them where they are. They need to know that God has not abandoned them. God is right there with them—hurting with them, weeping with them, ready to help, willing to provide grace and strength to get them through any situation. When your children see you seeking God for comfort and strength, they will also learn to rely on God's strength in tough times. Your faith can be a pivotal point in their healing.

If you are uncertain of how to start the necessary process of healing and reconciliation for your children, there are several avenues you might try. You can ask friends who have gone through a similar experience how they handled it with their children. Seek advice from your counselor, if you are seeing one, or your procurator. In the end, you are probably the one best qualified to know what will help your children; you know them better than anyone else. Pray about it, and trust your own instincts.

Above all, listen to them: listen with compassion, with sympathy, with love, and without judgment. Encourage them to talk. Give them permission to be angry. Hold them when they need comfort and reassurance. Help them understand that forgiveness—when they are ready—is not a feeling. It is a choice.

Teach your children that feelings like anger, hurt, disappointment, betrayal, and abandonment are all essential emotions, given to us by God. They serve the purpose of self-preservation. Once you have been hurt, you want to avoid situations in which you will be hurt again. Healthy self-love protects but does not imprison you in an isolated cocoon. Allow yourself and your children to express these emotions in a healthy way so that bitterness will not eat away at your lives. Emotions give you a sense of vulnerability; forgiveness gives you the courage and confidence to keep reaching out to others. Emotions make you human; forgiveness empowers you to rise above the frailties of humanity.

If you are going to teach your children to forgive as God forgives, you must learn from God how to forgive. Because you are not divine, you will probably not be able to completely forget offenses or offenders, but through God's divine grace you can swim in the waters of memory without drowning. When you choose to stop replaying the old memory tapes of despair and replace those destructive thoughts with good ones that come from God, your children will notice your change of attitude. Through your example of refusing bitterness and choosing God's strength, you will be giving your children the invaluable gift of hope.

Guide your children to hang on to God and the promises God gives. Read the Scriptures together, and meditate on their meaning. Use some of the verses from the previous chapter on closure, and encourage them, by your example, *to choose* to believe that what God says is true. By encouraging the faith of your children, you may find your own faith strengthened.

Spiritual growth is a lifelong and sometimes painful process of learning about salvation. Your annulment can be a part of this lifelong passage to maturity. Hold God's hand. Trust where God leads you. Rest in God's constant love.

And may the peace of Christ be with you.

Bibliography

Bateman, Lana L. *God's Crippled Children*. Dallas, TX: Philippian Ministries, 1985.

Blue, Ken. *Healing Spiritual Abuse: How to Break Free From Bad Church Experiences*. Downer's Grove, IL: InterVarsity Press, 1993.

Carter, Les. *Heartfelt Change: Turning Harmful Emotions into Positive Character*. Chicago: Moody Press, 1993.

Cooper, Rev. R. John. *The Advocate-Healer: A Primer for Healing During the Annulment Process*. Master's thesis for St. Mary Seminary, January 15, 1983.

Davis, Ron L. *The Healing Choice*. Waco, TX: Word Books, 1986.

Droege, Thomas A. *The Healing Presence: Spiritual Exercises for Healing, Wellness, and Recovery*. HarperSanFrancisco, 1992.

Ensley, Eddie. *Prayer That Heals Our Emotions*. San Francisco: Harper & Row, 1988.

Hassell, David. *Healing the Ache of Alienation: Praying Through and Beyond Bitterness*. New York: Paulist Press, 1990.

Klein, Allen. *The Healing Power of Humor: Techniques for Getting Through Loss, Setbacks, Upsets, Disappointments, Difficulties, Trials, Tribulations, and All That Not-so-funny Stuff*. Los Angeles: Jeremy P. Tarcher, Inc., distributed by St. Martin's Press, 1988.

Kostyu, Frank. *Healing Life's Sore Spots*. New York: Hawthorne Books, 1976.

Lewis, C. S. *A Grief Observed*. San Francisco: Broadman and Holman, 1999.

Linn, Matthew and Dennis. *Healing Life's Hurts: Healing Memories Through Five Stages of Forgiveness.* New York: Paulist Press, 1978.

_____ . *Healing of Memories.* New York: Paulist Press, 1984.

Linn, Matthew and Dennis, and Fabricant, Sheila. *Healing the Eight Stages of Life.* Mahwah, NJ: Paulist Press, 1988.

Lucado, Max. *A Gentle Thunder: Hearing God Through the Storm.* Dallas: Word Publications, 1995.

Luks, Allan with Payne, Peggy. *The Healing Power of Doing Good—the Health and Spiritual Benefits of Helping Others.* New York: Fawcett Columbine Press, 1992.

MacNutt, Francis. *The Power to Heal.* New York: Bantam, 1979.

Marsch, Michael. *Healing Through the Sacraments.* Collegeville, MN: Liturgical Press, 1989.

Oursler, Will. *The Healing Power of Faith.* New York: Berkley Books, 1991.

Robinson, Laura Jo. *"The Role of Forgiving in Emotional Healing: A Theological and Psychological Analysis."* Doctoral dissertation, Fuller Theological Seminary, School of Psychology, 1988.

Samra, Cal. *The Joyful Christ: The Healing Power of Humor.* San Francisco: Harper & Row, 1986.

Schlemon, Barbara Leahy. *Healing the Wounds of Divorce: a Spiritual Guide to Recovery.* Notre Dame, IN: Ave Maria Press, 1992.

Seamands, David. *Healing for Damaged Emotions.* Colorado Springs: Chariot Victor, 1998.

_____ . *Healing of Memories.* Wheaton, IL: Victor Books, 1985.

Ten Boom, Corrie. *The Hiding Place.* Old Tappan, NJ: Fleming H. Revell Co., 1971.

Tournier, Paul. *Guilt and Grace: a Psychological Study.* San Francisco: Harper, 1983.

Wilson, William. *The Grace to Grow: the Power* of *Christian Faith in Emotional Healing.* New York: Bantam, 1985.

Yancey, Phillip. Where Is God When It Hurts? Grand Rapids, MI: Zondervan Publishing House, 1990.

CPSIA information can be obtained
at www.ICGtesting.com
Printed in the USA
FFOW05n0838060214